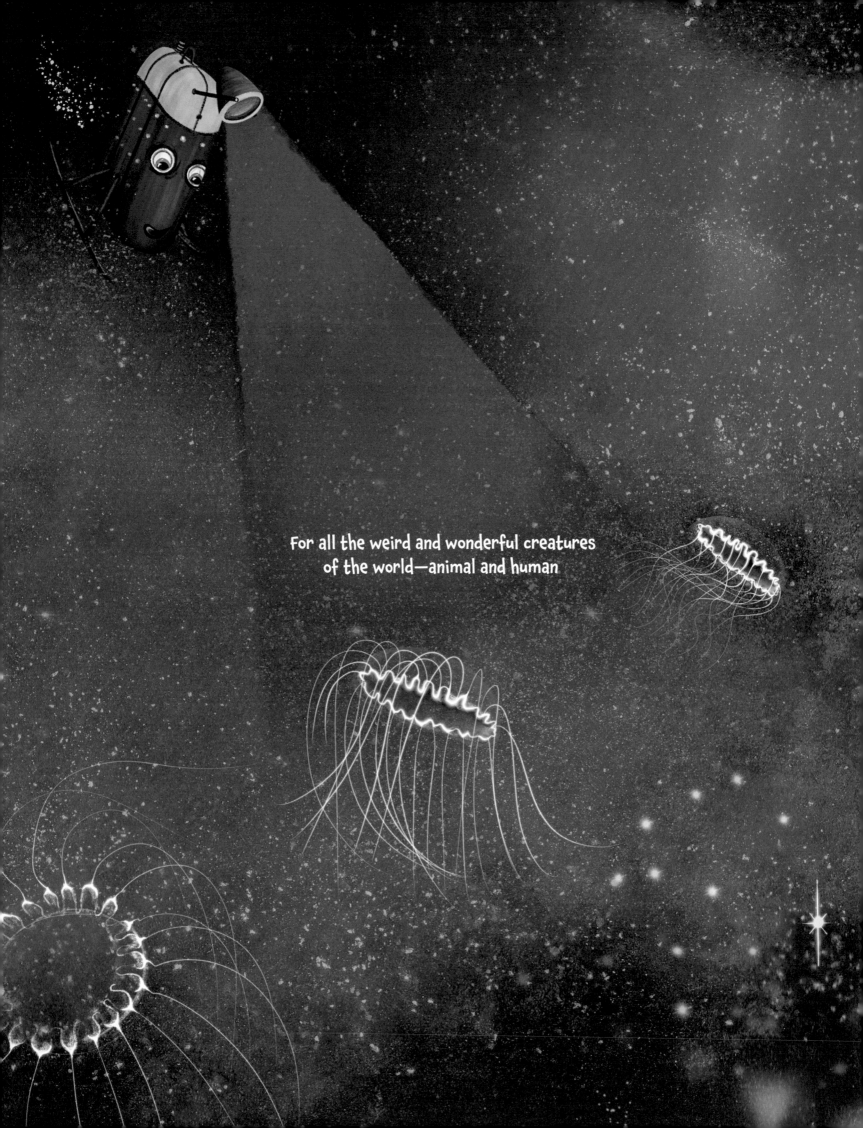

For all the weird and wonderful creatures
of the world—animal and human

WHERE THE WEIRD THINGS ARE

An Ocean Twilight Zone Adventure

Written by **Zoleka Filander**

with Woods Hole Institute for Oceanographic Science

Illustrations by **Patricia Hooning**

EARTHAWARE
KIDS

WOODS HOLE
OCEANOGRAPHIC
INSTITUTION

A voice wakes me up. "Ready to go?"
And then I'm lifted into the air and
lowered into something cold and wet.
"Good luck, little one,"
another voice calls as I start to sink.
Down, down, down, down . . .

It's getting colder and darker. And I can barely see anything anymore. Where am I? What am I doing here? I don't even know who I am. All I know is that I feel completely alone. **But wait!** Something's glowing in the distance.

A strange creature floats toward me
and peers at me with one yellow eye.

"Oh, hello," I say. "I noticed your lights. I have lights, too.
Could we be related? Like long-lost twins or something?"

"Highly unlikely," the creature replies. "I'm the amazing strawberry squid."

"I shimmer. I shine. I dazzle. I dance."

It comes closer, staring at me with its other eye, which is small and blue.

"Whoaaa! Weird!" I gasp.

"Nonsense! I am beyooootiful. Ask anyone. Well, anyone I don't eat, that is.
But you look nothing like a strawberry squid I'm afraid.
In fact, you're kind of weird yourself!" the squid says, jetting off.

Weird? Me?
Just then I feel something wrapping itself around my legs.
WHAT. IS. THAT?

"Who, me?" I ask.

The blob nods solemnly. "But if you stick with me, you'll be safe!
We Atolla jellyfish have an alarm system. Look!" Its whole body
suddenly flashes bright blue.

"Oooh! Let me try," I say, squeezing my eyes tight to
make my lights flash. "Anything?" I ask, opening one eye.

"Nope. Nada. Nothin'," the Atolla says.
"What kind of jellyfish did you say you were again?"

Suddenly there's a flicker of movement in the water.
"Look out!" the jellyfish shouts, flashing brightly.

"Wait!" I cry. But it's too late. The jellyfish is already gone.

SWOOOOOOOOSH!

A gigantic creature rushes by, sending me spinning.

"Hey!" I yell.

"Sorry," the creature says, "but I'm in a hurry to catch some tasty squid!"

"Oh! Can I come, too?"

"Not a good idea," the creature replies. "We swordfish work alone."

"Aww, why doesn't anyone want to hang out with me?" I ask. "Maybe I'm just too weird."

"Weird? Try having a sword for a nose," the swordfish calls, racing off.

I try to keep up, but it's gone in a flash. I stop, completely lost and alone again. What now?

Just then, I feel something slippery on me.

"Don't mind us, we're just tidying up," says a blob-like creature as it slides by. "We're salps, aka the **Ocean Clean-Up Gang**. We clean the water by eating and pooping."

"Nice to meet you," I reply. "I'm . . . well . . . I'm not sure **who** I am."

"That's weird," says the boss salp. "Why don't you hop on and join us? Just watch out for the poop. We've had a big lunch!"

All of a sudden, I spot a huge dark cloud coming right for us.

"What's that?" I ask, trembling.

"That's the Krill Squad," the boss salp explains. "Come on team. This patch of ocean's not big enough for the both of us."

I try to follow the salps. But before long I'm surrounded

. . . by thousands of tiny creatures with beady little eyes.

"Atten-shun!" one of them bellows. "You there! Look lively!"

"Who, me?" I ask. "But I'm not one of you . . . at least I don't think I am."

"Well, you sure don't look like a krill," the creature barks.
"But if you're going to hang around in these waters, you need to
get in formation. Lots of enemies out there. Whales, seals, birds,
all waiting to gobble us up! We've got to stick together.
Safety in numbers!"

"But there's only one of me," I say.

Suddenly, a terrifying set of fangs lunges out of the
darkness! I start to warn the krill but they're already
spiralling away.

SNAP!

"Ow! My **deeth!**" a creature yowls. "Your shell's so hard!"

"So are your fangs!" I say with a smile.

"Sorry," the creature says, looking a little ashamed. "I'm a fangtooth, by the way.
Hey, wanna see my party trick?"

The fangtooth opens its jaws wide, showing two rows of needle-sharp teeth.
Then it clamps its mouth shut again, hiding them completely.

The fangtooth laughs. "What's **your** party trick?"

"I don't think I have one," I sigh.

"That's weird," the fangtooth says with a shrug.
Just then, something swims by. "Ooh, lunch!" **CHOMP!**

I have to look away. And when I turn back, the fangtooth is gone.

There seems to be something special about everyone down here . . . except for me.

"Hey, what's tickling me?" I shout, spinning around.

Whatever it is, it has a body that seems to stretch on forever.
No, wait! It's actually hundreds of small creatures all joined together.

"We're a siphonophore, the longest organism around," one of them says proudly.

"Try saying that with a mouthful of crustaceans," another says with a giggle.

"Some of us are even longer than a blue whale!" adds a third.

"Wow!" I say. "Room for one more on board?"

"Sorry, too risky," the siphonophore says, slowly twisting away.
"We may be big, but we're fragile. You might break our chain."

Great. I'm too weird even for a siphonophore.

Just then, I spot a glow in the distance. It gets closer and closer . . .
until it lights up the sharpest, spiniest teeth I've **ever** seen!

"Fangtooth? Is that you?" I ask, hopefully.

"Nope. I'm an anglerfish," a kind voice answers. "Who are you?"

"I don't know," I sigh. "I'm not fast. I can't glow. I don't have a squad or fangs.
Even my light is boring compared to yours. I'm just weird."

The anglerfish chuckles and shines its light directly on me.
"Down here, everyone is different, but
everyone belongs. We're all a little weird.

And that's a GOOD thing!"

"So **weird** is good?" I ask.

The anglerfish smiles. "Of course!
Imagine if we were all the same?
Now **that** would be boring."

Just then, I feel myself rising
upward through the water.

Up, up, up, up, up, up, up, up, up, up

I blink as I hear a voice.

"Meso safely on deck!" the voice shouts.

Meso? Is that me? I wonder, feeling a little dazed.

"Time to get the schools to join online," the voice says.
"I bet they can't wait to see what Meso found down in
the weird and wondrous Ocean Twilight Zone!"

"Hello, students," the voice says, "I'm the chief scientist on this research vessel. And these are some of the sea creatures we met today."

"They're all so weird!" a student exclaims.

"Isn't it fantastic!" the scientist says. "It's called diversity. And thanks to Meso, our underwater explorer, we can learn even more about how it keeps our planet's ecosystems healthy—including human ones."

So that's who I am, Meso the underwater explorer!

"A fish with its own flashlight . . . a pink glowing squid . . . a super-pooping clean-up gang," another student says excitedly. "Cool!"

The scientist laughs. "Well, it's time to get Meso charged up for the next mission."

Another adventure?

I wonder where I'll be going this time . . .
and what creatures I'll meet.

All I know is I can't wait to go
where the wonderful weird things are!

Let's meet the **real-life creatures** that live in the Ocean Twilight Zone!

Mesobot

The Mesobot is an **underwater robot** that helps researchers learn more about the weird and wonderful creatures that live in the **Ocean Twilight Zone** (OTZ). It has a pair of small thrusters to move very quietly through the water, and it uses special lights and cameras to focus on individual creatures and study their behavior. Meso is able to collect small samples of plankton, microbes, and seawater, which it brings back to the surface to be studied.

Engineers designed the Mesobot so it couldn't really be flipped over by a swordfish like Meso is in our story!

Strawberry Squid

This squid gets its name from the strawberry-colored light cells called **photophores** that cover its skin. It also has asymmetrical eyes, with one large yellow one that looks upward and a smaller blue eye that looks downward. Its eyes are perfect for spotting snacks swimming by!

Atolla Jellyfish

The Atolla jellyfish is also known as the "**alarm jelly**." That's because it flashes bright blue light to startle its predators so it can escape. Not bad for a creature without a brain—or a digestive, respiratory, or central nervous system for that matter!

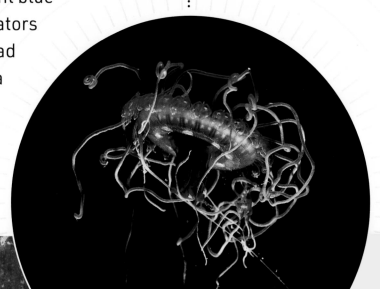

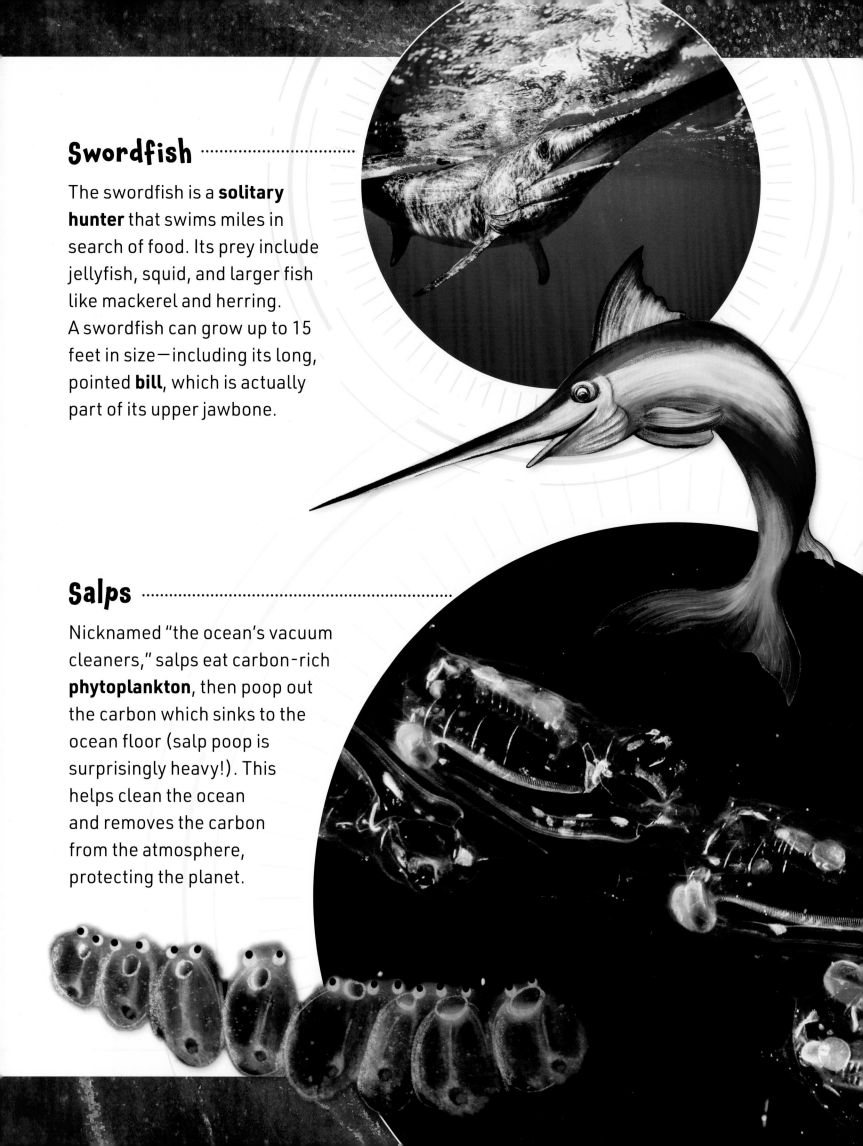

Swordfish

The swordfish is a **solitary hunter** that swims miles in search of food. Its prey include jellyfish, squid, and larger fish like mackerel and herring. A swordfish can grow up to 15 feet in size—including its long, pointed **bill**, which is actually part of its upper jawbone.

Salps

Nicknamed "the ocean's vacuum cleaners," salps eat carbon-rich **phytoplankton**, then poop out the carbon which sinks to the ocean floor (salp poop is surprisingly heavy!). This helps clean the ocean and removes the carbon from the atmosphere, protecting the planet.

Krill

At just 2.4 inches long, krill may be tiny but they're also a vital part of the **marine food chain**. To protect themselves from their many predators, they live together in large **swarms** of millions. The largest krill swarm ever was so big it could be seen from space!

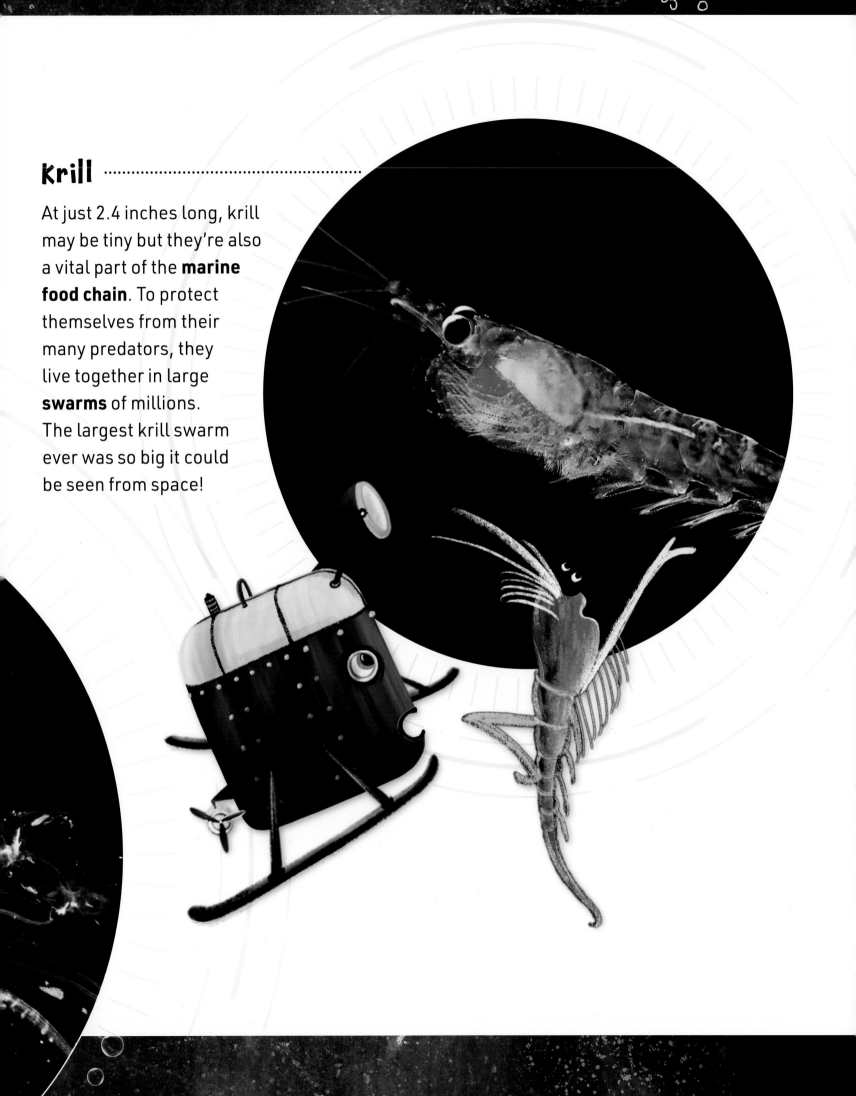

Fangtooth

The fangtooth has the **largest teeth** of any ocean creature relative to its body size. And even though it's only 6 inches long, it is the top predator in the OTZ. Their mouths have special **cavities** for their sharp fangs so they don't pierce their own skulls!

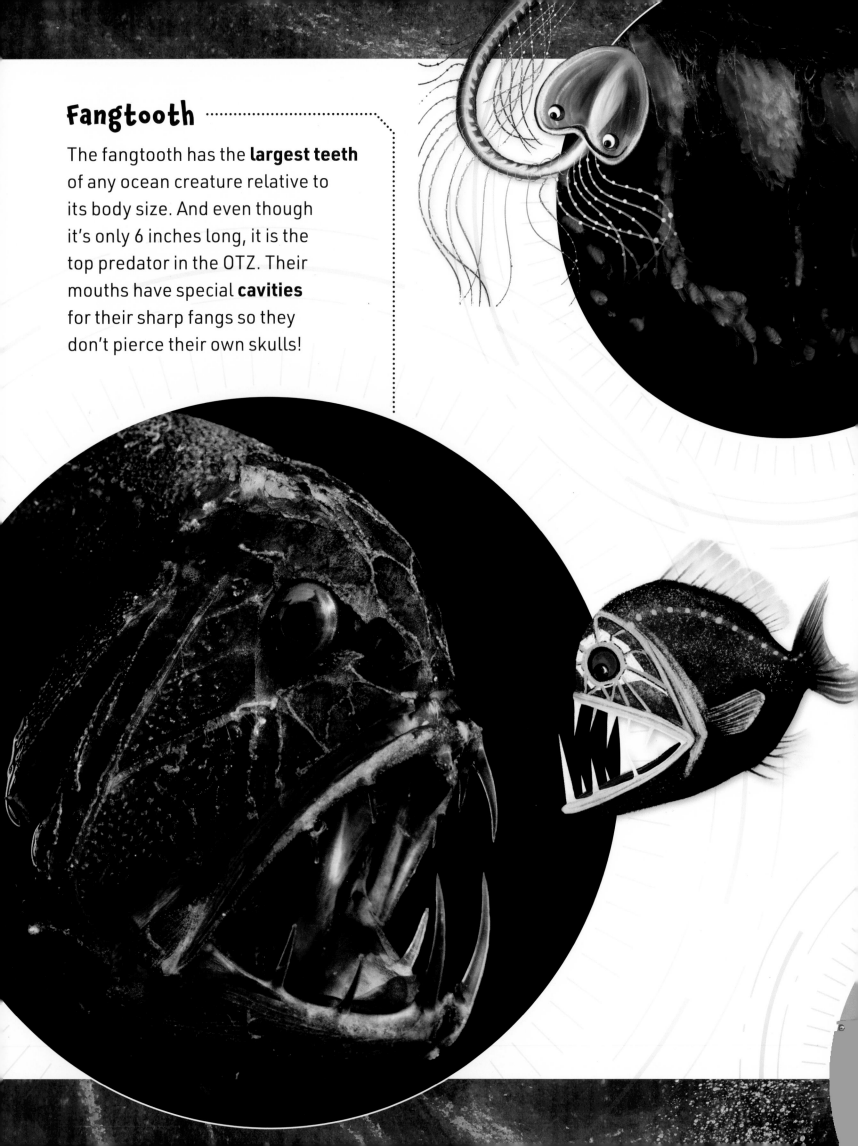

Siphonophores

Siphonophores may look like a large, single creature, but they're actually a **colony** of individual ones, all with highly specialized skills that work together. Siphonophores are the **longest organism** on the planet, with some having reached an incredible 150 feet!

Anglerfish

The female anglerfish has what looks like an **illuminated fishing pole** dangling from its forehead. Known as the **esca**, it's used to lure small fish and shrimp close enough to be eaten. Full of sharp teeth, an anglerfish's mouth is so big it can swallow prey twice its size!

The Team

Here are a few members of the real-life team, ready to take Mesobot on new adventures to the deep.

WHICH CREATURE ARE YOU?

Take the quiz and find out!

keepitweird.us

EARTHAWARE
KIDS

Published by EarthAware Kids
A subsidiary of Insight International, L.P.
PO Box 3088
San Rafael, CA 94912
www.insighteditions.com

 Find us on Facebook: www.facebook.com/InsightEditions
 Follow us on Twitter: @insighteditions

Library of Congress Cataloging-in-Publication Data available.

ISBN: 978-1-64722-588-9

Publisher: Raoul Goff
VP of Licensing and Partnerships: Vanessa Lopez
VP of Creative: Chrissy Kwasnik
VP of Manufacturing: Alix Nicholaeff
VP, Editorial Director: Vicki Jaeger
Associate Publisher: Sara Miller
Art Director: Stuart Smith
Editorial Assistant: Elizabeth Ovieda
Senior Production Editor: Jan Neal
Senior Production Manager: Greg Steffen
Senior Production Manager, Subsidiary Rights: Lina s Palma-Temena

Printed in China by Insight Editions
10 9 8 7 6 5 4 3 2 1

The Publisher would like to thank Maria Wilhelm for her invaluable help bringing this project forward and Samuel Harp for his partnership and support in creating an exceptional book.

WOODS HOLE
OCEANOGRAPHIC
INSTITUTION

Special thanks to The Audacious Project, Craig and Susan McCaw Foundation, OceanX, Happel Foundation, James Family Charitable Trust, National Science Foundation, Robertson Foundation, and Generous Anonymous Donors for their generous support for the Ocean Twilight Zone Project at Woods Hole Oceanographic Institution.

ROOTS of PEACE   REPLANTED PAPER

Insight Editions, in association with Roots of Peace, will plant two trees for each tree used in the manufacturing of this book. Roots of Peace is an internationally renowned humanitarian organization dedicated to eradicating land mines worldwide and converting war-torn lands into productive farms and wildlife habitats. Roots of Peace will plant two million fruit and nut trees in Afghanistan and provide farmers there with the skills and support necessary for sustainable land use.

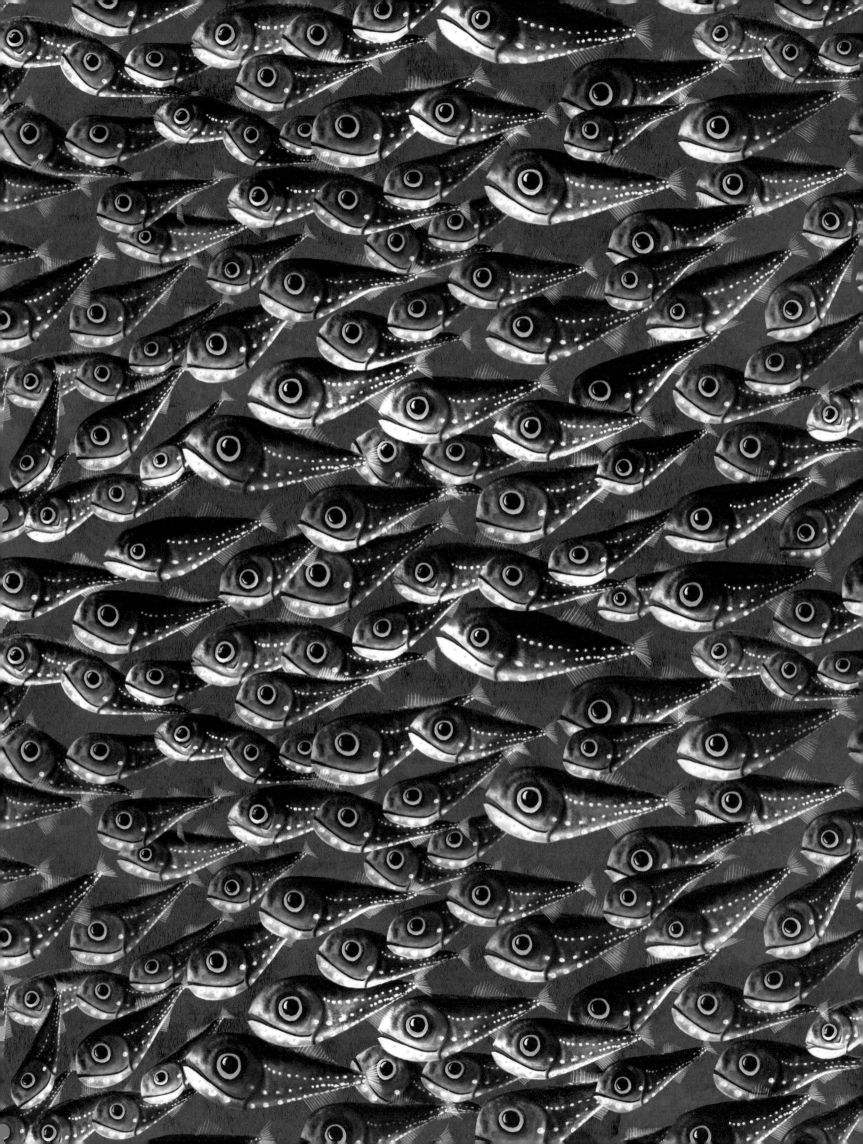